The Ultimate Christmas Treasury

The Ultimate Christmas Treasury

Heartwarming Stories, Festive Recipes, and Timeless Traditions for a Magical Holiday

LINDSEY T. GORDON

The Ultimate Christmas Treasury

COPYRIGHT

All rights reserved. No part of this publication may be reproduced, distributed, or transmitted in any form or by any means, including photocopying, recording, or other electronic or mechanical methods, without the prior written permission of the publisher, except in the case of brief quotations embodied in critical reviews and certain other noncommercial uses permitted by copyright law.

Copyright © Lindsey T. Gordon, 2024.

The Ultimate Christmas Treasury

TABLE OF CONTENTS

INTRODUCTION..................................**8**
  The Spirit of Christmas: A Season of Joy and Connection............................8
    Why Christmas Traditions Matter..9
    How This Book Will Enrich Your Holiday Experience........................10

CHAPTER ONE............................**13**
  The Origins of Christmas........................13
    The Birth of Christmas Traditions Around the World................................15
    How Christmas Evolved Through the Centuries.................................. 18

CHAPTER TWO............................**22**
  Heartwarming Christmas Stories... 22
    Modern Stories of Christmas Miracles...24
    Personal Reflections on the True Meaning of Christmas........................27

The Ultimate Christmas Treasury

CHAPTER THREE..........................30
  Festive Recipes to Share the Joy..30
    Traditional Holiday Meals from Around the World............................30
    Sweet Treats: Christmas Cookies, Cakes, and More............................. 33
    Creative Recipes for a Contemporary Christmas Feast... 36

CHAPTER FOUR............................40
  Timeless Christmas Traditions............. 40
    Decorating the Christmas Tree: A Symbol of Unity..............................40
    The Rituals of Giving and Receiving Gifts................................... 43
    Carols, Concerts, and Music to Celebrate the Season.........................46

CHAPTER FIVE..............................50
  DIY Christmas Crafts and Decorations...50
    Handmade Ornaments: Adding a Personal Touch................................. 50

The Ultimate Christmas Treasury

    Creative Wrapping Ideas for Memorable Gifts.............. 53
    Festive Home Décor on a Budget.............. 57

CHAPTER SIX.............. 61
    Christmas Around the World.............. 61
    Unique Celebrations in Europe.............. 61
    Christmas Traditions in Asia and Africa.............. 65
    How America Blends Multicultural Holiday Practices.............. 68

CHAPTER SEVEN.............. 73
    The Magic of Santa Claus.............. 73
    The History and Legends of Saint Nicholas.............. 74
    How the Santa Myth Continues to Captivate Children.............. 83

CHAPTER EIGHT.............. 87
    Giving Back During the Holidays.............. 87
    Acts of Kindness: Stories of Holiday Generosity.............. 88

The Ultimate Christmas Treasury

Volunteering Opportunities for
Families and Individuals.................. 92
How to Incorporate Charitable
Giving Into Your
Celebrations.. 97

CHAPTER NINE............................ 103
Christmas Entertainment.................... 103
Iconic Christmas Movies for All
Ages.. 104
Festive Games to Play with
Friends and Family......................... 112
Books That Capture the Holiday
Spirit... 116

CHAPTER TEN.............................. 121
Planning the Perfect Christmas........... 121
Time Management Tips for a
Stress-Free Holiday........................ 122
Budgeting for Gifts, Décor, and
Events... 126
Creating a Personalized
Christmas Checklist....................... 131

CONCLUSION................................ 137
Reflecting on the Holiday
Season... 137

The Ultimate Christmas Treasury

Reflecting on the Holiday Season 138
Carrying the Spirit of Christmas Throughout the Year 140
A Final Wish for a Joyful and Magical Holiday 144

The Ultimate Christmas Treasury

INTRODUCTION

The Spirit of Christmas: A Season of Joy and Connection

Christmas is more than just a day on the calendar; it's a feeling that transcends time and geography. It's a season that unites people in celebration, reminding us of the value of love, generosity, and togetherness. For centuries, Christmas has been a beacon of joy, offering a reprieve from the routines of everyday life and a chance to reconnect with loved ones.

The spirit of Christmas is evident in the twinkling lights that adorn our homes, the laughter of children as they await Santa's arrival, and the aroma of freshly baked cookies wafting through the air. But perhaps the most profound aspect of this season is the sense of connection it fosters. Whether it's through sharing a meal, exchanging heartfelt gifts, or simply spending time together, Christmas has an unparalleled ability to bring people closer.

Why Christmas Traditions Matter

Traditions are the heart of Christmas. They ground us in shared experiences, linking generations past and present through rituals that create a sense of continuity and belonging. Whether it's hanging ornaments that have been in the family for decades, singing carols by the fireplace, or baking a secret family recipe, these practices become the threads that weave together the fabric of the holiday season.

But why do traditions hold such importance? On a personal level, they provide stability and a sense of identity, especially in an ever-changing world. On a societal level, they serve as a reminder of shared values like love, peace, and goodwill. Traditions also offer a unique opportunity for families to create lasting memories. Children who eagerly participate in these rituals today often carry them forward, ensuring their preservation for future generations.

How This Book Will Enrich Your Holiday Experience

The Ultimate Christmas Treasury is more than just a collection of stories, recipes, and tips—it's a comprehensive guide designed to deepen your appreciation for the season and

The Ultimate Christmas Treasury

enhance every aspect of your holiday. Whether you're a seasoned Christmas enthusiast or someone looking to rekindle the magic, this book is your companion for creating a truly memorable celebration.

Each chapter is crafted to provide inspiration, practical advice, and heartwarming tales that capture the essence of Christmas. You'll find:

1. Stories that remind you of the true meaning of the season, whether they're timeless classics or modern accounts of holiday miracles.

2. Recipes that bring the flavors of Christmas to your table, from traditional dishes to innovative

The Ultimate Christmas Treasury

creations for a contemporary celebration.

3. Traditions that honor the past while offering fresh ideas to make the season uniquely yours.

4. Crafts and Decorations that transform your home into a festive wonderland without breaking the bank.

By the end of this book, you'll have all the tools you need to make this Christmas the most magical yet. Whether your goal is to create unforgettable memories with your loved ones, discover new traditions, or simply find joy in the little things, this treasury is here to guide you every step of the way.

The Ultimate Christmas Treasury

CHAPTER ONE

The Origins of Christmas

The origins of Christmas trace back thousands of years, long before the birth of Jesus Christ. Many elements of the modern holiday are rooted in ancient pagan festivals that celebrated the winter solstice, a time when days began to lengthen and light returned to the earth.

In ancient Rome, the festival of Saturnalia, held in mid-December, honored Saturn, the god of agriculture. This week-long celebration was characterized by feasting, gift-giving, and a reversal of social roles where slaves were temporarily treated as equals.

Similarly, the Yule festival, celebrated by the Germanic and Nordic peoples, marked the rebirth of the sun. Yule traditions included lighting fires, feasting, and decorating homes with evergreens—symbols of life enduring through winter's harshness. These customs were later integrated into Christmas celebrations, with the Yule log and evergreen decorations becoming enduring symbols of the season.

When Christianity began to spread, early Church leaders sought to replace these pagan celebrations with a Christian holiday. By the 4th century, December 25 was officially designated as the feast day of Christ's birth, aligning it with existing solstice festivals.

The Ultimate Christmas Treasury

This strategic choice helped ease the transition from paganism to Christianity while preserving beloved seasonal traditions.

The Birth of Christmas Traditions Around the World

As Christianity spread across the globe, different cultures infused their own customs into the celebration of Christmas, creating a rich tapestry of traditions that vary widely by region.

1. Europe: In Victorian England, Charles Dickens' A Christmas Carol played a significant role in shaping modern Christmas customs. This era emphasized family gatherings, festive meals, and charity. In Germany, the Christmas tree tradition, or

Tannenbaum, became central to the holiday. Germans also introduced the Advent calendar, a countdown to Christmas Day filled with treats or small gifts.

2. Latin America: Countries like Mexico celebrate Las Posadas, a reenactment of Mary and Joseph's search for shelter. This nine-day festival culminates in joyous feasts and piñatas. In Puerto Rico, parrandas (musical caroling parties) bring communities together, spreading holiday cheer with traditional instruments and songs.

3. Asia and Africa: In Japan, where Christmas is more secular, it has

become a time for couples to celebrate romance, often with a special meal. Meanwhile, in Ethiopia, where Christmas is called Ganna, celebrations on January 7 (based on the Julian calendar) include fasting, prayer, and communal feasts.

4. North America: The United States and Canada have embraced a melting pot of traditions, from decorating homes with lights to enjoying Santa Claus, whose modern image was popularized by 19th-century artist Thomas Nast.

These regional traditions highlight the adaptability of Christmas, showing how it evolves to reflect the unique cultural values and histories of those who celebrate it.

How Christmas Evolved Through the Centuries

The celebration of Christmas has undergone significant changes throughout history, shaped by religious, cultural, and social influences.

1. The Middle Ages: By the early medieval period, Christmas was a significant religious feast in Europe, marked by church services and solemn reflection. However, it was also a time of revelry, with elements of feasting and merrymaking carried over from pagan traditions. Lords hosted grand banquets, and villagers engaged in wassailing—a precursor to modern caroling.

2. The Reformation Era: In the 16th and 17th centuries, the Protestant Reformation led to a decline in Christmas celebrations in some regions. Puritans in England and America even banned the holiday, deeming it too pagan and frivolous. However, Christmas persisted in Catholic countries and eventually resurged in popularity.

3. The Victorian Revival: The 19th century was a turning point for Christmas, largely thanks to Queen Victoria and Prince Albert, who popularized the German tradition of decorating Christmas trees in England. Writers like Charles Dickens also helped transform Christmas into

The Ultimate Christmas Treasury

a family-centered, charitable holiday. His story A Christmas Carol reminded readers of the importance of generosity and goodwill, themes that remain central to the season today.

4. The Modern Era: The 20th century saw the commercialization of Christmas, with the rise of department store Santas, greeting cards, and the Coca-Cola ads that solidified Santa's jolly image. However, the essence of Christmas—celebrating love, family, and hope—remains intact.

Today, Christmas continues to evolve. With the rise of globalization, many cultures adopt elements of the holiday while blending them with their own traditions.

Technology has also transformed how we celebrate, from virtual holiday greetings to online shopping for gifts. Yet, no matter how it changes, Christmas endures as a time of reflection, celebration, and connection.

This chapter invites readers to see Christmas not just as a single day but as a culmination of centuries of traditions, stories, and shared human experiences.

CHAPTER TWO

Heartwarming Christmas Stories

For centuries, Christmas stories have captured the magic of the season, often conveying timeless messages of love, generosity, and redemption. These classic tales remain beloved across generations, reminding us of the enduring power of storytelling to ignite the holiday spirit.

1. Charles Dickens' A Christmas Carol
   Perhaps the most famous Christmas story, A Christmas Carol tells the tale of Ebenezer Scrooge, a miserly man transformed by the visits of three ghosts on Christmas Eve. Through its vivid characters and moral lessons, Dickens' masterpiece underscores the

importance of compassion, charity, and embracing the joy of the season.

2. The Gift of the Magi by O. Henry
   This short story illustrates the selfless love of a young couple who sacrifice their most prized possessions to buy each other meaningful gifts. Despite their humble circumstances, their acts of generosity exemplify the true spirit of Christmas: giving from the heart.

3. The Nutcracker and the Mouse King by E.T.A. Hoffmann
   This whimsical tale, which inspired the famous ballet, follows young Clara as she embarks on a magical journey with her Nutcracker prince. Filled with wonder and enchantment, the

story evokes the childlike joy and imagination often associated with Christmas.

These classics, though steeped in the traditions of their times, resonate with universal themes that remain relevant today. They serve as a reminder that the true magic of Christmas lies in acts of kindness, selflessness, and love.

Modern Stories of Christmas Miracles

While classic tales lay the foundation for the season's literary traditions, modern stories continue to capture the spirit of Christmas, often reflecting contemporary themes and challenges.

The Ultimate Christmas Treasury

1. The Polar Express by Chris Van Allsburg

   This beautifully illustrated children's book follows a young boy on a magical train ride to the North Pole. The story emphasizes the importance of belief, even in the face of doubt, and captures the wonder of Christmas through a child's eyes.

2. One Day in December by Josie Silver

   A modern romance set against the backdrop of the holiday season, this novel explores themes of fate, friendship, and love. It highlights how Christmas can be a time for serendipity and new beginnings.

3. Real-Life Accounts of Christmas Miracles

From stories of strangers paying off layaway items in stores to miraculous reunions of loved ones, real-life acts of kindness during the holidays remind us that miracles don't have to be grand to be meaningful. These modern miracles, often shared in news outlets and on social media, reflect the spirit of giving and hope that defines the season.

These contemporary tales show how Christmas continues to inspire new narratives, bringing fresh perspectives to the holiday's enduring themes of love, generosity, and magic.

Personal Reflections on the True Meaning of Christmas

While stories from literature and modern media provide inspiration, personal experiences often resonate the most deeply. Reflecting on our own Christmas memories helps us connect with the holiday's core values and find meaning in the traditions we hold dear.

1. Family Memories

    For many, the true meaning of Christmas is found in simple, heartfelt moments shared with loved ones. These might include decorating the tree together, baking cookies with a grandparent, or gathering around the fireplace to tell stories. Such memories often become cherished traditions

The Ultimate Christmas Treasury

passed down through generations.

2. Acts of Kindness and Generosity

One of the most profound aspects of Christmas is the joy of giving. Whether it's donating to a charity, volunteering at a shelter, or surprising a neighbor with a thoughtful gift, these acts of kindness embody the spirit of the season. Personal reflections on giving often reveal how these gestures, however small, create lasting impact for both the giver and recipient.

3. Moments of Reflection and Gratitude

The hustle and bustle of the holidays can sometimes overshadow its deeper meaning. Personal reflections often highlight the importance of pausing to

The Ultimate Christmas Treasury

appreciate the blessings of the season—family, health, and the opportunity to celebrate together. These quiet moments of gratitude are where the true magic of Christmas often resides.

This chapter invites readers to explore the many ways Christmas stories—whether classic, modern, or personal—enrich the season. Through these tales and reflections, we are reminded that the heart of Christmas lies not in material gifts, but in the connections, memories, and love we share.

CHAPTER THREE

Festive Recipes to Share the Joy

Christmas and food are inseparable, with festive meals and treats being central to holiday celebrations worldwide. Cooking for Christmas is more than preparing sustenance; it's an act of love that brings families together, bridges cultures, and creates cherished memories. This chapter celebrates the joy of holiday cooking with a collection of traditional, indulgent, and modern recipes that make the season truly magical.

Traditional Holiday Meals from Around the World

Christmas feasts reflect the rich cultural diversity of the world. Across continents, families gather to enjoy dishes that carry deep-rooted traditions and flavors.

1. United Kingdom: Roast Turkey with All the Trimmings

   A centerpiece of British Christmas dinners, roast turkey is served with stuffing, cranberry sauce, and gravy. Side dishes like roasted potatoes, Brussels sprouts, and Yorkshire pudding complete this hearty meal. For dessert, Christmas pudding—steamed and often flambéed with brandy—is a must.

2. Italy: Feast of the Seven Fishes

   An Italian-American tradition, this feast features seven seafood dishes, symbolizing the number of sacraments in Catholicism. Popular dishes include fried calamari, linguine with clams, and baccalà (salted cod). Panettone, a sweet bread with dried fruit, is often served for dessert.

3. Mexico: Tamales and Pozole

    Mexican Christmas meals often include tamales, corn dough filled with meats or cheese, and wrapped in corn husks. Pozole, a hominy stew with pork or chicken, is another staple, garnished with lime, radishes, and lettuce. Buñuelos, crispy fried dough coated in cinnamon sugar, provide a sweet finish.

4. Sweden: Julbord (Christmas Smorgasbord)

The Swedish Christmas table features an array of dishes, including pickled herring, gravlax (cured salmon), meatballs, and Janssons Frestelse (a creamy potato casserole). Saffron buns and glögg (spiced mulled wine) add festive warmth.

By recreating these traditional dishes, families can embark on a culinary journey that connects them to the global spirit of Christmas.

Sweet Treats: Christmas Cookies, Cakes, and More

No Christmas celebration is complete without an array of delectable sweets. From cookies to cakes, these confections bring joy to all who partake.

The Ultimate Christmas Treasury

1. Classic Christmas Cookies

    a. Gingerbread Men: Spiced with cinnamon, ginger, and cloves, these cookies are perfect for decorating with royal icing.
    b. Sugar Cookies: These buttery treats can be cut into festive shapes and adorned with colorful sprinkles or icing.
    c. Peppermint Bark Cookies: A modern twist combining chocolate, crushed candy canes, and cookie bases for a minty delight.
2. Traditional Christmas Cakes

    a. Fruitcake: A dense cake filled with dried fruits, nuts, and spices, often soaked in rum or brandy for weeks to enhance its flavor.

b. Yule Log (Bûche de Noël): A chocolate sponge cake rolled with cream and decorated to resemble a log, symbolizing the Yule tradition.

3. Other Sweet Treats

a. Stollen: A German sweet bread filled with marzipan and dried fruit, dusted with powdered sugar.

b. Torrone: Italian nougat candy made with almonds, honey, and egg whites, perfect for gifting or enjoying after meals.

> c. Hot Cocoa Bombs: A contemporary favorite, these chocolate spheres melt in hot milk to reveal marshmallows and cocoa mix.

Baking these treats is an opportunity to bond with loved ones, especially children, who delight in decorating cookies or sampling dough.

Creative Recipes for a Contemporary Christmas Feast

While traditional recipes honor the past, modern interpretations keep the holiday table exciting. Creative dishes bring innovation to Christmas feasts while maintaining the season's spirit of indulgence.

The Ultimate Christmas Treasury

1. Reimagined Main Courses

    a. Herb-Crusted Salmon: A lighter yet festive alternative to turkey, perfect for a health-conscious Christmas dinner.
    b. Vegetarian Wellington: A savory pastry filled with mushrooms, lentils, and spinach, catering to plant-based guests.
    c. Honey-Glazed Duck: An elegant centerpiece offering a rich, flavorful twist to the holiday meal.
2. Modern Sides

    a. Maple-Roasted Vegetables: A medley of carrots, parsnips, and

Brussels sprouts caramelized with maple syrup and pecans.
  b. Truffle Mashed Potatoes: Creamy potatoes infused with truffle oil for a luxurious upgrade.
  c. Cranberry-Orange Quinoa Salad: A refreshing dish combining quinoa, dried cranberries, orange zest, and walnuts.
3. Innovative Desserts

  a. Christmas Cheesecake: Swirled with peppermint or spiced with eggnog, this dessert brings festive flair to a classic favorite.
  b. Frozen Hot Chocolate Pie: A no-bake treat combining hot

chocolate mix and whipped cream in a graham cracker crust.
c. Spiced Pear Galette: A rustic pastry featuring pears, cinnamon, and a hint of ginger.

These creative recipes encourage culinary experimentation, ensuring every guest finds something to savor.

This chapter celebrates the diversity of Christmas cooking, from cherished family recipes to modern creations. By exploring these festive dishes, readers can transform their holiday tables into a feast of joy, warmth, and connection. Whether you're cooking for a small gathering or hosting a grand celebration, these recipes embody the delicious magic of the season.

CHAPTER FOUR

Timeless Christmas Traditions

Christmas traditions are the heart of the holiday season, providing a sense of continuity, community, and joy. These customs, passed down through generations, help us connect to the deeper meaning of the holiday and to one another. From the glittering Christmas tree to the joyful melodies of carols, timeless traditions enrich the spirit of Christmas and keep its magic alive year after year.

Decorating the Christmas Tree: A Symbol of Unity

The Christmas tree is one of the most iconic symbols of the holiday season, standing as a beacon of unity and celebration in homes around the world. Its origins date back to ancient pagan practices, where evergreens symbolized life and resilience during the dark winter months.

1. A Historical Tradition

    The modern Christmas tree tradition began in Germany during the 16th century when devout Christians brought decorated trees into their homes. Martin Luther, the Protestant reformer, is often credited with first adding candles to a tree to replicate the twinkling stars he saw in the night sky.

    In the 19th century, Queen Victoria and Prince Albert popularized the Christmas tree in England, and the tradition quickly spread across Europe and to the Americas. Today, it is a universal symbol of Christmas cheer.

2. Modern-Day Practices

Decorating the tree has become a cherished family ritual, often accompanied by holiday music, laughter, and hot cocoa. Each ornament tells a story—handmade decorations, heirlooms passed down through generations, or baubles collected on travels. The act of decorating is not merely about aesthetics; it is a moment of connection, reflection, and shared joy.

3. Tree-Lighting Ceremonies

Public tree-lighting ceremonies have

also become a hallmark of the season, uniting communities in celebration. Iconic events like the lighting of the Rockefeller Center Christmas Tree in New York City draw thousands of spectators and millions of viewers worldwide, encapsulating the spirit of togetherness.

The Christmas tree, whether grand or humble, embodies the values of family, hope, and unity that define the holiday season.

The Rituals of Giving and Receiving Gifts

Gift-giving is one of the most anticipated aspects of Christmas, rooted in the biblical story of the Magi bringing gold, frankincense, and myrrh to the Christ child. Over time, this act of generosity evolved into a widespread tradition, symbolizing love and appreciation for others.

1. Historical Origins

    In early Christian Europe, Saint Nicholas, the patron saint of children, became a central figure in gift-giving traditions. His legendary acts of charity inspired the modern-day Santa Claus, whose image as a jolly gift-bearer was popularized in the 19th century.

2. The Joy of Giving

    The true essence of Christmas gifting lies in the thought and care behind each present. It is not about extravagance but about showing loved ones that they are cherished. Handmade gifts, personalized tokens, or simply wrapping a gift with care can make the gesture even more meaningful.

3. Gift-Giving Rituals Around the World

    a. United States: Families exchange gifts on Christmas morning, often guided by lists sent to Santa Claus.

    b. Spain: Gifts are traditionally given on January 6, Epiphany, to honor the arrival of the Magi.

    c. Japan: While Christmas is not a religious holiday, gift-giving has become a way to show appreciation among friends and colleagues.

The exchange of gifts is not merely a transaction; it is a ritual that fosters gratitude, strengthens bonds, and spreads happiness during the holiday season.

Carols, Concerts, and Music to Celebrate the Season

Music is the soul of Christmas, capturing the joy, nostalgia, and spirituality of the season. From ancient carols to contemporary hits, Christmas music bridges generations and brings people together in celebration.

1. The Origins of Christmas Carols
   Carols date back to medieval Europe, where they were originally festive

songs sung during all seasons. By the 13th century, carols became closely associated with Christmas, often performed in churches and public squares. Classics like Silent Night and O Come All Ye Faithful have endured for centuries, embodying the reverence and beauty of the holiday.

2. Community and Family Traditions

Caroling is a beloved tradition where groups of singers travel door to door, spreading cheer with festive songs. This practice fosters a sense of community, with neighbors coming together to celebrate. Families often have their own musical traditions, such as playing favorite Christmas albums while decorating the tree or

The Ultimate Christmas Treasury

gathering around a piano for sing-alongs.

3. Modern Celebrations of Music

   a. Christmas Concerts: From school performances to grand orchestral productions like Handel's Messiah, Christmas concerts bring people together to enjoy the magic of live music.
   b. Iconic Songs: Modern classics like Mariah Carey's All I Want for Christmas Is You and Bing Crosby's White Christmas have become staples of the season.
   c. Streaming Playlists: Today's technology allows us to curate personalized playlists, blending

traditional carols with contemporary hits to create the perfect holiday soundtrack.

Music is a universal language that transcends cultural and linguistic barriers, making it an integral part of Christmas celebrations worldwide.

This chapter highlights the timeless nature of Christmas traditions, from the glowing Christmas tree to the joy of giving and the power of music to unite. These rituals, whether practiced individually or communally, weave together the fabric of the holiday season, ensuring its magic endures for generations to come.

CHAPTER FIVE

DIY Christmas Crafts and Decorations

Creating your own Christmas crafts and decorations is one of the most enjoyable ways to immerse yourself in the holiday spirit. Whether you're designing handmade ornaments, experimenting with gift wrapping, or crafting budget-friendly décor, DIY projects allow you to express creativity, bond with loved ones, and add a personal touch to your holiday celebrations.

Handmade Ornaments: Adding a Personal Touch

Ornaments are the soul of the Christmas tree, and making them by hand infuses the holiday with warmth and individuality. Whether simple or elaborate, handmade ornaments become keepsakes that tell stories and evoke memories year after year.

1. Classic DIY Ornaments

    a. Salt Dough Ornaments: Combine flour, salt, and water to create a dough that can be shaped into festive designs. Bake them, paint them, and seal with varnish for long-lasting tree decorations.
    b. Pinecone Ornaments: Gather pinecones from outside, add a touch of glitter, and tie them with ribbons for rustic yet elegant charm.
    c. Photo Ornaments: Insert small family photos into clear plastic

or glass ornaments for a sentimental touch. These make wonderful gifts as well.

2. Eco-Friendly Ornaments

   a. Dried Citrus Slices: Thinly slice oranges or lemons, dry them in the oven, and string them with twine for an all-natural, fragrant decoration.
   b. Recycled Paper Stars: Fold old magazines or wrapping paper into stars, trees, or snowflakes, giving new life to materials otherwise discarded.
   c. Fabric Scraps and Yarn: Use leftover textiles to create soft,

colorful ornaments that bring a cozy aesthetic to your tree.

3. Ornaments as Family Activities

Making ornaments can be a family tradition, with each member contributing their unique designs. Whether it's painting, gluing, or assembling, the process creates shared moments of laughter and connection that are just as cherished as the finished product.

Creative Wrapping Ideas for Memorable Gifts

Gift wrapping is an art that transforms presents into delightful surprises. Going beyond standard store-bought paper, creative wrapping ideas make your gifts

The Ultimate Christmas Treasury

stand out while reflecting your personality and thoughtfulness.

1. Personalized Wrapping Techniques

    a. Hand-Stamped Paper: Use stamps and ink to create custom designs on plain kraft paper. Snowflakes, stars, and trees are easy and festive motifs.
    b. Calligraphy Tags: Write names or holiday wishes in elegant calligraphy on tags, giving each gift a sophisticated and personalized flair.
    c. DIY Gift Bags: Sew or glue fabric scraps into reusable gift bags, which double as an eco-friendly alternative to paper.

The Ultimate Christmas Treasury

2. Nature-Inspired Wrapping

    a. Evergreen Sprigs and Pinecones: Tuck small branches or pinecones into ribbons or twine for a rustic, earthy feel.
    b. Cinnamon Sticks and Dried Flowers: Add these fragrant and colorful accents to make your gifts visually stunning and aromatic.
    c. Brown Paper with Twine: A classic and minimalist choice that pairs well with natural embellishments.
3. Interactive Wrapping Ideas

a. Scavenger Hunt Tags: Add clues to tags leading to another gift or a surprise location.
b. Decorative Boxes: Use sturdy, reusable boxes decorated with festive designs or themes.
c. Embedded Extras: Attach small keepsakes, such as ornaments or candy canes, to the exterior of the gift for an added touch.

These creative techniques not only enhance the presentation of your gifts but also show your recipients that their gifts were prepared with care and attention.

Festive Home Décor on a Budget

Decking your halls for Christmas doesn't have to break the bank. With a little ingenuity, you can create stunning decorations that rival store-bought items while saving money and reducing waste.

1. DIY Wreaths and Garlands

    a. Natural Wreaths: Use a wire frame and forage for evergreens, holly, and berries to create a lush wreath. Add ribbons or ornaments for extra flair.
    b. Paper Garland: Cut snowflakes, stars, or other shapes out of colored paper and string them together for a charming and inexpensive garland.
    c. Popcorn and Cranberry Strings: A timeless craft that doubles as

decoration for the tree or mantel.

2. Upcycled Decorations

    a. Jar Lanterns: Turn mason jars into festive lanterns by filling them with fairy lights, fake snow, or small ornaments.

    b. Wine Bottle Centerpieces: Paint old wine bottles in metallic hues and use them as vases for holiday greenery.

    c. CD Ornaments: Repurpose old CDs by cutting them into shapes and hanging them as reflective ornaments.

3. Simple Yet Striking Accents

a. Candle Displays: Arrange pillar candles of varying heights on a tray with sprigs of greenery and pinecones for an elegant centerpiece.
b. DIY Snow Globes: Fill glass jars with water, glitter, and small holiday figurines for a whimsical display.
c. Ribbon-Wrapped Staircase: Wrap your staircase banister with wide ribbons, intertwining them with fairy lights or greenery for an eye-catching effect.

Budget-friendly décor often brings a more personal touch to your home, as each piece carries the satisfaction of having been lovingly crafted.

This chapter encourages readers to embrace the joy of creativity during the holiday season. From crafting ornaments to reimagining gift wrapping and home décor, DIY projects add heart and soul to Christmas celebrations. These hands-on activities not only beautify your surroundings but also provide opportunities for bonding, mindfulness, and self-expression, ensuring your holiday is as unique and memorable as you are.

CHAPTER SIX

Christmas Around the World

Christmas is a global celebration, but its traditions and customs are as diverse as the cultures that observe it. While the spirit of love, joy, and generosity ties these celebrations together, the ways in which different regions mark the holiday reflect unique histories, beliefs, and local flavors. This chapter takes readers on a journey through Christmas festivities across continents, offering a glimpse into the vibrant tapestry of global holiday traditions.

Unique Celebrations in Europe

Europe is the birthplace of many Christmas traditions, and its celebrations are steeped in history, folklore, and festivity. Each

The Ultimate Christmas Treasury

country brings its own charm to the holiday season.

1. Germany: The Land of Christmas Markets

    Germany is synonymous with enchanting Christmas markets, or Weihnachtsmärkte. These festive gatherings fill town squares with twinkling lights, the scent of mulled wine (Glühwein), and stalls selling handmade gifts, ornaments, and traditional foods like bratwurst and stollen. Advent calendars and wreaths also originated in Germany, marking the countdown to Christmas.

2. Sweden: The Feast of Saint Lucia

    Celebrated on December 13, Saint

Lucia's Day is a highlight of the Swedish Christmas season. A young girl dressed in a white gown and wearing a crown of candles leads a procession, symbolizing the return of light during the darkest time of year. Families enjoy saffron buns (lussekatter) and other traditional treats.

3. Italy: La Befana and Nativity Scenes

    Italian Christmas revolves around the Nativity scene (presepe), with intricate, hand-crafted displays in homes and churches. Another unique figure is La Befana, a kind-hearted witch who delivers gifts to children on January 6, Epiphany. The Feast of the Seven Fishes, celebrated on Christmas

Eve, is a hallmark of Italian holiday cuisine.

4. Spain: Las Posadas and the Three Kings

Spanish Christmas begins with Las Posadas, a reenactment of Mary and Joseph's search for shelter. On January 6, Día de los Reyes (Three Kings' Day) is the main day for gift-giving, marked by parades and feasting on Roscón de Reyes, a sweet bread with hidden surprises inside.

Europe's rich history and diverse cultures ensure that Christmas is celebrated with deep tradition and joy.

Christmas Traditions in Asia and Africa

Although Christianity is not the predominant religion in many parts of Asia and Africa, Christmas is celebrated with unique cultural adaptations, blending local customs with Christian practices.

1. The Philippines: Simbang Gabi and Giant Lanterns

    The Philippines holds the world's longest Christmas season, beginning in September and lasting through January. One of the most cherished traditions is Simbang Gabi, a series of pre-dawn masses leading up to Christmas. The Giant Lantern Festival in San Fernando showcases elaborate, colorful lanterns (parols) that symbolize the Star of Bethlehem.

2. Japan: A Season of Light and Romance

In Japan, Christmas is a secular celebration marked by dazzling light displays and romantic dinners. Families often enjoy a "traditional" Christmas meal of fried chicken, popularized by a KFC marketing campaign in the 1970s. Christmas Eve is seen as a day for couples, akin to Valentine's Day, while Christmas Day is quieter.

3. Africa: Vibrant and Community-Centered Celebrations

Across Africa, Christmas is a time for community and worship. In Ethiopia

The Ultimate Christmas Treasury

and Eritrea, Christmas (Genna) is celebrated on January 7 with traditional games and a feast after church services. In South Africa, Christmas coincides with summer, and families gather for outdoor braais (barbecues). Midnight carols and colorful dances are integral parts of the festivities.

4. India: Midnight Mass and Mango Leaf Décor

In India, Christians decorate their homes with mango leaves and light small clay lamps. Midnight Mass is the highlight of the season, followed by festive meals featuring curries, rice, and sweets like kul-kuls. Large cities like Goa and Mumbai host vibrant parades and street celebrations.

Asia and Africa bring unique energy and creativity to Christmas, blending local traditions with the universal message of the holiday.

How America Blends Multicultural Holiday Practices

The United States, known as a melting pot of cultures, celebrates Christmas with traditions that reflect its rich diversity. Each community contributes its unique customs, creating a vibrant mosaic of holiday practices.

1. European Influences in American Christmas

   Many American Christmas traditions

trace their roots to European immigrants. The Christmas tree, stockings hung by the chimney, and Santa Claus all have origins in European folklore. German settlers popularized Advent calendars, while Dutch traditions introduced the concept of Saint Nicholas, which evolved into Santa Claus.

2. Hispanic Celebrations: Las Posadas and Nochebuena

Hispanic communities in the U.S. bring lively customs like Las Posadas, reenacting Mary and Joseph's journey. Nochebuena (Christmas Eve) is often celebrated with a grand feast, featuring tamales, lechón (roast pork), and desserts like flan. Midnight Mass,

The Ultimate Christmas Treasury

or Misa de Gallo, is an essential part of the celebration.

3. African-American Traditions: Christmas and Kwanzaa

For many African-American families, Christmas overlaps with Kwanzaa, a week-long celebration honoring African heritage and unity. Music, storytelling, and feasts bring communities together, enriching the holiday season with cultural pride. Gospel music and church gatherings play a central role in the Christmas experience.

4. Asian-American Contributions

Asian-American communities incorporate their heritage into

The Ultimate Christmas Treasury

Christmas festivities. Filipino-Americans celebrate Simbang Gabi, while Korean-Americans blend traditional holiday feasts with Korean dishes like kimchi and bulgogi. Chinese-American families might enjoy dim sum or a hot pot meal on Christmas Day.

America's Christmas celebrations reflect its multicultural identity, showcasing how the holiday can be both deeply personal and universally shared.

This chapter reveals the rich diversity of Christmas celebrations worldwide, illustrating how the holiday adapts to different cultures while maintaining its essence of love, joy, and generosity.

The Ultimate Christmas Treasury

By exploring these global traditions, readers can find inspiration to incorporate new elements into their own celebrations, making their Christmases even more meaningful and inclusive.

CHAPTER SEVEN

The Magic of Santa Claus

Santa Claus is perhaps the most beloved and universally recognized figure associated with Christmas. His jolly persona, red suit, and reindeer-powered sleigh have captured the imagination of children and adults alike for centuries. But behind the image of the man who delivers gifts to children around the world lies a fascinating history, rich with folklore, legends, and cultural evolution.

This chapter delves into the story of Santa Claus, tracing his origins, his magical helpers, and the enduring impact of the Santa myth on the holiday season.

The History and Legends of Saint Nicholas

The modern-day Santa Claus has roots in the historical figure of Saint Nicholas, a 4th-century bishop from the city of Myra, in what is now Turkey. Saint Nicholas was known for his kindness, generosity, and miracles, particularly in his care for children and the poor. Over time, his legend evolved into the figure we now recognize as Santa Claus, but his story has taken many forms across different cultures.

1. Saint Nicholas: The Bishop of Generosity

    Saint Nicholas was born in the late 3rd century and became known for his acts of charity and compassion. He is said to have secretly given gifts to the poor, including a legendary story where he provided dowries for three sisters so they could avoid being sold into slavery. Saint Nicholas' acts of kindness made him a beloved figure, and after his death, he was canonized as the patron saint of children, sailors, and merchants.

Saint Nicholas' feast day, celebrated on December 6, became an important day for gift-giving in many European cultures, particularly in countries like the Netherlands and Germany. The image of the benevolent bishop evolved into a more secular, gift-bringer figure, especially in places like the United States.

The Ultimate Christmas Treasury

2. The Transformation into Santa Claus

The transformation of Saint Nicholas into the modern Santa Claus can be traced to Dutch settlers in New York, who brought their tradition of Sinterklaas to the American colonies. In the early 19th century, the name Santa Claus emerged from a phonetic adaptation of Sinterklaas. Washington Irving's 1809 work A History of New York introduced the character of Santa Claus as a jovial, pipe-smoking figure who traveled on a sleigh.

In the mid-19th century, the poem A Visit from St. Nicholas (better known as The Night Before Christmas) further shaped the image of Santa Claus, describing him as a "jolly old elf" with a belly that "shook like a bowl full of jelly" and a sleigh pulled by eight reindeer. The poem's depiction solidified many of the traits we associate with Santa today.

3. Coca-Cola and the Final Touches

In the 1930s, Coca-Cola's holiday advertisements played a pivotal role in solidifying Santa Claus' iconic image. The brand hired artist Haddon Sundblom to create a series of cheerful, red-suited, white-bearded Santa images for its Christmas campaigns, cementing the cheerful, plump version of Santa we know today.

The Ultimate Christmas Treasury

The history of Santa Claus is a rich tapestry of religious legend, cultural traditions, and commercial influence, each layer adding to the enduring magic of his character.

Santa's Helpers: Reindeer, Elves, and More Santa Claus is rarely seen without his trusted helpers, who bring even more magic to the holiday season. These companions, including his reindeer, elves, and Mrs. Claus, help bring Santa's myth to life, contributing to the sense of wonder that surrounds the Christmas season.

1. The Reindeer: Santa's Flying Companions

    The eight reindeer who pull Santa's sleigh are among the most famous animals in folklore. In The Night

Before Christmas, the names of Santa's reindeer—Dasher, Dancer, Prancer, Vixen, Comet, Cupid, Donder (sometimes spelled "Thunder"), and Blitzen—are introduced. These names are thought to be derived from the characteristics of reindeer, known for their agility and strength in northern climates.

   a. Rudolph the Red-Nosed Reindeer: In 1939, the story of Rudolph, the ninth reindeer, was introduced by Robert L. May in a booklet created for Montgomery Ward department store. Rudolph's glowing red nose helps guide Santa's sleigh through foggy nights, making him an essential part of Santa's team. Rudolph quickly became a beloved part of the Christmas narrative, immortalized in songs, movies, and merchandise.

2. Santa's Elves: The Unsung Heroes of Christmas

Santa's elves are the hardworking, magical creatures responsible for crafting toys and preparing gifts in Santa's North Pole workshop. Elves have been a part of Christmas folklore for centuries, but their role in Santa's story became more defined in the 19th century.

In modern depictions, elves are often shown as small, merry beings who work tirelessly to prepare for Christmas Eve. They wear pointy hats, green and red clothes, and are known for their cheerful demeanor. Santa's elves are portrayed as the true backbone of the operation, tirelessly ensuring that each child receives a special gift.

> a. The North Pole Workshop: In stories, Santa's elves reside in the North Pole, a magical and remote place where time seems to stand still. This fantastical workshop is often depicted as bustling with activity—an expansive space filled with toy-making machines, gift

wrapping stations, and large quantities of festive supplies.

3. Mrs. Claus: Santa's Loving Partner

While Santa is the star of the show, Mrs. Claus plays an equally important role in the Christmas narrative. She is often depicted as a kind, nurturing figure who helps Santa prepare for his journey on Christmas Eve. In many stories, Mrs. Claus is the one who ensures Santa stays fed, rested, and ready for the big night. Though she does not always appear in every Christmas tale, Mrs. Claus is often seen as an emblem of the warmth and kindness that Christmas represents.

Together, Santa's helpers create a magical, whimsical world where every detail is meticulously planned and every gift is made with care. The imagery of reindeer soaring through the sky, elves working in unison, and Mrs. Claus ensuring everything runs smoothly enriches the myth of Santa Claus, giving children (and adults) a deeper sense of wonder.

How the Santa Myth Continues to Captivate Children

The myth of Santa Claus is one of the most enduring and enchanting stories in the world, captivating the imaginations of children for generations. The magic of Santa is not just in the idea of receiving gifts but in the belief in a world where kindness, generosity, and joy take center stage.

1. The Magic of Belief

   For children, the idea that Santa Claus knows their wishes, travels the world in a single night, and delivers presents to every good child is an incredibly powerful story. The mystery and wonder surrounding Santa—how he knows whether you've been naughty or nice, how he fits down chimneys, and how his reindeer can fly—sparks the imagination and makes Christmas feel truly magical.

2. Creating Lasting Memories

   The tradition of Santa Claus is often passed down within families, with parents playing an integral role in fostering the magic of the myth. Writing letters to Santa, leaving out cookies and milk, and hearing stories of Santa's journey create cherished memories that children carry with them into adulthood. The belief in Santa fosters a sense of wonder and excitement that makes Christmas feel like a time of pure joy.

3. Santa's Role in Teaching Values

Santa Claus also plays an important role in teaching children about the values of kindness, generosity, and selflessness. The concept of the "naughty or nice" list encourages children to behave well, and the idea of giving gifts encourages them to think of others. In this way, Santa is not just a figure of fantasy but a moral guide, encouraging positive behaviors while promoting the joy of giving during the holiday season.

Santa Claus remains a beloved and magical figure because he embodies the essence of Christmas: a time of joy, love, and hope. His story, rooted in history but continually evolving with new legends and tales, continues to inspire generations, keeping the spirit of Christmas alive in the hearts of children around the world.

This chapter explores the enduring allure of Santa Claus, from his origins as Saint Nicholas to the magical helpers who make Christmas Eve possible. Santa's myth is not just a story of gift-giving, but a timeless symbol of generosity, love, and the joy of believing in something magical.

CHAPTER EIGHT

Giving Back During the Holidays

The holiday season is not only a time for receiving gifts, but also a time for reflecting on the true meaning of Christmas—love, compassion, and generosity. While many celebrate by exchanging presents and enjoying festive meals, there is also a profound opportunity to give back to others.

Acts of kindness, volunteering, and charitable donations can transform the holiday season into something more meaningful, deepening our sense of community and making the world a little brighter for those in need. This chapter explores the importance of giving during the holidays and provides practical ways to share your blessings with others, helping to make the season truly special for everyone.

Acts of Kindness: Stories of Holiday Generosity

Generosity is at the heart of the Christmas spirit. Throughout history, there have been countless stories of individuals and communities going out of their way to spread kindness and help those less fortunate. These stories remind us that even the smallest acts of kindness can have a profound impact.

1. The Story of the Christmas Truce
   One of the most remarkable stories of holiday generosity occurred during World War I, when soldiers from opposing sides put down their

weapons and came together to celebrate Christmas. In December 1914, on the Western Front, soldiers on both sides of the trenches spontaneously called a ceasefire. They sang carols, exchanged gifts, and even played soccer in no-man's land. This Christmas Truce stands as a powerful example of how, even in the midst of conflict, the spirit of goodwill can unite people.

2. The Gift of the Magi

A classic tale of selfless love and sacrifice, "The Gift of the Magi" by O. Henry tells the story of a young couple, Jim and Della, who sacrifice their most treasured possessions to buy a Christmas gift for each other.

Della sells her long, beautiful hair to buy a chain for Jim's pocket watch, while Jim sells his watch to buy a comb for Della's hair. Both gifts become useless, but the sacrifices they make for each other exemplify the true meaning of giving during the holidays—love and selflessness over material gain.

3. Real-Life Stories of Giving Back

In modern times, many individuals and families share their blessings with those less fortunate. One story involves a group of neighbors who organize a "Secret Santa" program each Christmas. They anonymously purchase gifts for families who are struggling financially, ensuring that children have presents under the tree. This simple yet powerful act of generosity has become a cherished tradition in their community. Similarly, a woman in a small town noticed a homeless man near a bus stop each holiday season. One year, she decided to provide him with a Christmas meal and a warm blanket. Word spread, and soon others joined in, making sure he had everything he needed during the winter. These acts of kindness demonstrate how the Christmas spirit can inspire individuals to make a difference in the lives of others.

These stories highlight that the act of giving—whether through material gifts, time, or love—can transcend the holiday season, leaving lasting effects on both the giver and the receiver.

Volunteering Opportunities for Families and Individuals

Volunteering during the holidays is one of the most meaningful ways to give back to your community. Not only does it help those in need, but it also strengthens the bonds between family members and fosters a deeper sense of gratitude. This section explores various volunteer opportunities that are perfect for individuals and families, regardless of age or experience.

1. Soup Kitchens and Food Banks
    Many families choose to volunteer at local soup kitchens, food pantries, or

shelters. These places often experience a surge in demand during the holiday season, and they welcome the help of volunteers to prepare meals, sort food donations, or serve those in need. For example, the Salvation Army and Feeding America are two organizations that organize large-scale holiday food drives and meal services for homeless individuals or low-income families. These volunteer opportunities not only help provide meals but also allow volunteers to connect with people in their community who are facing hardship.

2. Holiday Toy Drives

Donating time to help organize or distribute toys to children in need is a holiday tradition for many families. Organizations like Toys for Tots and local community centers often run toy drives, where families can either donate new toys or volunteer to wrap and deliver gifts to children who might otherwise not receive anything. This volunteer activity is especially rewarding for families with children, as it teaches young ones about the joy of giving and helps them understand the importance of helping others.

3. Visiting Senior Citizens or Hospitalized Patients

Many elderly individuals and hospital patients spend the holidays alone, away from their families and loved ones. A simple visit, whether to an assisted living home, nursing facility, or hospital, can bring warmth and cheer to someone who might otherwise be isolated. Organizations like Meals on Wheels often rely on volunteers to deliver meals to homebound seniors, ensuring they have food and companionship during the holidays. For families with young children, organizing a caroling session or crafting homemade cards and gifts to distribute to seniors can be an especially meaningful way to engage children in the spirit of giving.

4. Homeless Shelters and Winter Clothing Drives

In colder climates, homelessness becomes an especially urgent issue during the winter months. Many homeless shelters are in need of extra hands to provide warmth and support to those without homes. Families can donate or volunteer to distribute winter coats, gloves, hats, and blankets to those living on the streets. They can also help shelters by serving meals, packing care packages, or assisting with emergency housing programs.

5. Adopt a Family or Elderly Person for Christmas

Many organizations run programs where families can "adopt" someone in need during the holiday season. These programs allow families to buy gifts, provide a holiday meal, or offer other forms of support to families or individuals who are struggling financially. The joy of seeing the happiness of others when they receive the support is often a deeply rewarding experience.

Volunteering during the holidays not only helps those in need but also teaches valuable lessons about compassion, empathy, and gratitude. It also creates lasting memories for families, as they come together to make a difference in their community.

How to Incorporate Charitable Giving Into Your Celebrations

Incorporating charitable giving into your holiday celebrations not only makes the season brighter for others but also reinforces the values of kindness and generosity. Here are some practical ways to ensure that giving back becomes an integral part of your holiday traditions.

1. Incorporate Giving Into Gift-Giving Traditions

    One simple way to give back during the holidays is by incorporating charitable giving into your gift exchange. Families can choose to donate to a favorite charity on behalf of a loved one or purchase gifts from fair-trade or charity-driven stores. Some families opt for "giving gifts of experience" rather than material items—such as making a donation to a cause that a family member is passionate about or volunteering together for a day of service.

2. Create a Giving Tree

A Giving Tree is a wonderful way to engage children in charitable giving. A tree or display is set up in the home, and instead of receiving gifts, family members can contribute items to donate to others. For example, children can place warm clothing, toiletries, or food in the tree, and those items can then be donated to local shelters or food banks. This tradition can become a meaningful ritual, teaching the values of generosity and selflessness.

3. Host a Charity-Focused Holiday Party

Instead of hosting a typical holiday

party with gifts and meals, consider hosting a "Charity Christmas Party." Encourage guests to bring donations of food, clothing, or money for a cause, rather than traditional gifts. Some families even invite guests to a "potluck-style" gathering, where they bring homemade meals that can be distributed to shelters or families in need. By combining celebration with charity, you help spread the joy of the season while supporting those in need.

4. Sponsor a Holiday Fundraiser

Many organizations hold holiday fundraisers to support specific causes, whether it's for children's hospitals, animal shelters, or homeless families. Families and friends can come together to fundraise for a cause close to their hearts. By contributing to a larger cause, individuals can feel connected to their community and the world beyond their doorstep.

This chapter emphasizes that Christmas is not only about receiving but also about giving. Through volunteering, charitable donations, and acts of kindness, we can make the holiday season brighter for those who need it most.

Whether through small gestures or large-scale community efforts, the holiday season provides a powerful opportunity to make a lasting difference in the lives of others. By incorporating giving into our celebrations, we deepen our connection to

The Ultimate Christmas Treasury

the true spirit of Christmas and help spread joy, peace, and love throughout the world.

CHAPTER NINE

Christmas Entertainment

The holiday season is not only a time for reflection, giving, and community, but it is also an opportunity for endless entertainment that brings joy to all. From classic movies that have become integral parts of the season to festive games that bring laughter to family gatherings, Christmas entertainment holds a special place in the hearts of many.

This chapter explores the best ways to celebrate through entertainment, including iconic Christmas movies, fun holiday games, and timeless books that capture the spirit of Christmas.

The Ultimate Christmas Treasury

Iconic Christmas Movies for All Ages

Movies have become an essential part of the Christmas experience, with classic films providing both nostalgia and new traditions for families. From heartwarming stories to comedies and animated features, these films offer something for everyone, helping to capture the magic of the season.

1. Classic Christmas Movies

    Some Christmas films have become essential viewing for families every December. These timeless classics often revolve around the themes of generosity, family unity, and holiday magic, teaching important lessons while spreading festive cheer.

a. It's a Wonderful Life (1946): This film is one of the most beloved Christmas classics. It tells the story of George Bailey, a man who is shown by an angel what life would be like if he had never been born. With its powerful message of community, love, and the value of one person's life, It's a Wonderful Life continues to resonate with viewers of all ages.

b. A Christmas Carol (various versions): Charles Dickens' tale of Ebenezer Scrooge has been adapted into countless films, television specials, and even stage performances. The story of

Scrooge's transformation from a miserly, cold-hearted man to a generous, compassionate soul has been retold in numerous ways, from the 1951 version starring Alastair Sim to the 2009 animated feature starring Jim Carrey. The themes of redemption and the Christmas spirit are ever-relevant.

c. Miracle on 34th Street (1947): A heartwarming story about a department store Santa who claims to be the real Santa Claus, this movie explores the themes of belief, innocence, and the magic of Christmas. Whether it's the original 1947 version or the

1994 remake, Miracle on 34th Street remains a holiday favorite.

2. Animated Christmas Movies

Animated films offer a colorful, imaginative way to tell Christmas stories, often aimed at younger audiences while still appealing to adults. These films are perfect for family viewing and create lasting memories.

   a. The Polar Express (2004): Based on the beloved children's book by Chris Van Allsburg, The Polar Express is an animated journey to the North Pole, where a young boy experiences the magic of

Christmas through an extraordinary train ride. With its stunning visuals and memorable music, it's a film that captures the wonder and enchantment of the holiday season.

b. A Charlie Brown Christmas (1965): This iconic animated special remains a favorite for families worldwide. The story of Charlie Brown trying to find the true meaning of Christmas amid the commercialism of the season resonates with both children and adults. With its jazz score by Vince Guaraldi and its timeless message about the value of kindness and understanding, it is a must-watch every Christmas.

c. How the Grinch Stole Christmas (1966): Based on Dr. Seuss' beloved book, this animated special has become a Christmas classic, with the Grinch's eventual transformation from a heart two sizes too small to one full of love and holiday spirit still captivating audiences after decades.

3. Modern Christmas Comedies

Modern Christmas comedies bring a fresh twist to holiday entertainment, often mixing humor with heartfelt moments to create the perfect balance

The Ultimate Christmas Treasury

for family viewing. These films are known for their charm, wit, and memorable moments.

- a. Home Alone (1990): The story of Kevin McCallister, a young boy accidentally left home alone while his family vacations, has become a cultural touchstone. As Kevin outwits two burglars, his adventure becomes an emblem of independence, bravery, and the importance of family. The slapstick humor, unforgettable lines, and holiday themes have made Home Alone an enduring Christmas classic.

b. Elf (2003): Starring Will Ferrell as Buddy the Elf, this modern holiday comedy combines silliness with warmth, showing how one person's infectious holiday spirit can change the lives of those around them. Buddy's journey to New York City to find his biological father is full of laughter, love, and lessons on embracing the holiday spirit.

c. Love Actually (2003): A romantic comedy set during Christmas, Love Actually intertwines the stories of multiple characters, all experiencing different aspects of love, loss, and hope. This film, often considered one of the best modern Christmas movies, provides a mix of humor, emotion, and seasonal magic.

Festive Games to Play with Friends and Family

Christmas is a time for gathering with loved ones, and playing games can help make these moments even more memorable. Whether you're hosting a large family reunion or enjoying an intimate holiday celebration, these games bring people together, creating lasting memories and plenty of laughs.

The Ultimate Christmas Treasury

1. Christmas Charades

   A holiday twist on the classic game of charades, Christmas Charades involves acting out Christmas-themed words, phrases, or actions. Players can choose from topics such as Christmas movies, holiday songs, or even common Christmas traditions like decorating the tree or building a snowman. This game works for all ages and can be played in teams or individually, making it perfect for family gatherings.

2. Holiday Pictionary

   Like charades, Pictionary is a fun and engaging drawing game where players attempt to draw a word or phrase for their team to guess. Holiday

The Ultimate Christmas Treasury

Pictionary can be personalized with holiday-themed words such as "snowflake," "reindeer," or "Santa's sleigh." It's a fantastic way to get everyone involved, and the drawings are sure to bring laughter as the holiday spirit fills the room.

3. Christmas Bingo

Christmas Bingo is a great way to keep younger guests entertained. Create bingo cards filled with Christmas images or words (e.g., Santa, snowman, Christmas tree, candy cane) and hand them out to players. Use a set of holiday-themed tokens or candy to mark the cards as the caller calls out the corresponding words or images. The first player to get five in a row wins a prize. This game is fun, easy to set up, and ensures everyone has a festive time.

4. Pin the Nose on Rudolph

A Christmas variation of the classic Pin the Tail on the Donkey, this game involves players attempting to pin a red nose onto a large poster of Rudolph the Reindeer while blindfolded. It's a fun, silly activity that's especially great for younger children, bringing excitement and laughter to any holiday celebration.

5. Christmas Scavenger Hunt

Organize a Christmas-themed scavenger hunt where players must find holiday items hidden around the house or yard. You can create a list of holiday-themed clues or riddles for them to follow, or give them a list of items to find, such as a stocking, a candy cane, a bell, and a snow globe. This game gets everyone moving and exploring, ensuring a fun-filled, festive time.

Books That Capture the Holiday Spirit

Books have long been a source of entertainment and inspiration during the holiday season, offering readers stories that evoke the magic of Christmas. Whether you're reading aloud with your family or enjoying a quiet moment by the fire, these books capture the essence of Christmas and its many joys.

The Ultimate Christmas Treasury

1. The Polar Express by Chris Van Allsburg

   A beautifully illustrated book that tells the story of a young boy who embarks on a magical train ride to the North Pole, The Polar Express captures the enchantment and wonder of Christmas. With its themes of belief, adventure, and the magic of Christmas, this book is a perfect read for children and adults alike.

2. A Christmas Carol by Charles Dickens

   A must-read classic, A Christmas Carol tells the story of Ebenezer Scrooge and his transformation from a miserly old man to a warm-hearted benefactor after being visited by the ghosts of Christmas Past, Present, and

The Ultimate Christmas Treasury

Yet to Come. This novella has inspired countless adaptations, but the original story remains a powerful reminder of the true meaning of Christmas—kindness, generosity, and redemption.

3. How the Grinch Stole Christmas by Dr. Seuss

Dr. Seuss' beloved tale of the Grinch, who learns the true meaning of Christmas after attempting to steal it, is a holiday favorite for readers of all ages. Its catchy rhymes, whimsical illustrations, and heartwarming message make it a timeless book for children and a nostalgic one for adults.

The Ultimate Christmas Treasury

4. The Snowman by Raymond Briggs

    This wordless picture book tells the enchanting story of a boy who builds a snowman that comes to life and takes him on a magical adventure. With its beautiful illustrations and magical atmosphere, The Snowman has become a favorite Christmas read, capturing the wonder and fleeting beauty of the holiday season.

5. The Best Christmas Pageant Ever by Barbara Robinson

    This humorous and heartwarming story tells the tale of the Herdman siblings, known for being the "worst kids in the history of the world," who take over the church's Christmas pageant. Through their wild antics and

The Ultimate Christmas Treasury

unexpected transformation, the story shows how even the most unlikely people can experience the true meaning of Christmas.

This chapter celebrates the entertainment that makes the Christmas season so special. From the timeless charm of holiday movies to the laughter-filled games and books that convey the magic of the season, Christmas entertainment plays a key role in creating cherished memories and bringing loved ones closer together.

Whether you're cuddling up to watch a favorite movie or playing a lively game with friends and family, the entertainment of Christmas helps make the season bright.

CHAPTER TEN

Planning the Perfect Christmas

The holiday season is often filled with joy, but it can also come with its fair share of stress. From decorating the house to purchasing gifts, hosting events, and coordinating family gatherings, the list of things to do can seem overwhelming.

However, with the right planning and organization, you can ensure that your Christmas is not only memorable but also stress-free. This chapter offers practical time management strategies, budgeting tips, and personalized checklists to help you plan the perfect Christmas without the chaos.

Time Management Tips for a Stress-Free Holiday

The key to a stress-free holiday season is proper planning. With so many tasks to accomplish, it's easy to feel frazzled, but breaking things down into manageable steps can make a huge difference. Here are some effective time management strategies to ensure you stay organized and enjoy the festive season without unnecessary stress.

1. Start Early

    One of the best ways to minimize holiday stress is to start your planning as early as possible. The earlier you begin, the more time you'll have to tackle each task at a comfortable pace. For instance, start planning your holiday meals and shopping lists in

November, so you have time to order special items, compare prices, or check out sales. If you're sending holiday cards, consider addressing them early in the month to avoid the last-minute rush.

2. Create a Calendar

Whether it's a physical planner, a digital calendar, or a project management app, having a visual schedule is key. Mark key dates, such as holiday parties, family visits, and school breaks, then work backward from these events to ensure that everything is done in time. Schedule small tasks over the course of several days to avoid cramming everything into one frantic weekend. For example, set aside one evening to wrap gifts, another to bake cookies, and a third to decorate the tree. Breaking tasks into manageable chunks ensures you don't feel overwhelmed.

3. Prioritize Your Tasks

It's easy to get caught up in the holiday rush, but not everything on your list is equally important. Prioritize tasks by their level of importance and urgency. For instance, purchasing gifts may take precedence over decorating the house, or organizing family travel plans may be more urgent than holiday baking. Identify what absolutely needs to be done and tackle those tasks first, leaving the less urgent ones for later. This helps reduce the pressure of having everything done at once.

4. Delegate and Ask for Help

Christmas planning is not a one-person job. Don't hesitate to delegate tasks to family members or friends, whether it's having the kids help decorate the house, asking your partner to handle the grocery shopping for the holiday meal, or organizing a family member to wrap gifts. Getting everyone involved in the holiday preparations not only lightens the workload but also creates a sense of teamwork and family bonding.

5. Set Realistic Expectations

   Remember, perfection is not the goal. Christmas is about enjoying the time with your loved ones and making memories, not about having every detail just right. It's important to set realistic expectations about what can and cannot be done. If something doesn't turn out as planned, don't stress—embrace the imperfections. After all, it's the joy and love of the season that truly matters, not the perfectly executed holiday events.

Budgeting for Gifts, Décor, and Events

While the holidays are a time for generosity and celebration, they can also be financially stressful if you don't keep track of your spending. From buying gifts for family and friends to decorating your home and planning holiday events, costs can quickly add up. Creating a clear and manageable budget is essential to ensure that you don't start the New Year with unnecessary debt or financial worries.

    1. Set a Budget for Gifts

        Gift-giving is one of the most important aspects of Christmas, but it's easy to go overboard if you're not careful. Start by determining how much you want to spend on gifts this year. Then, make a list of everyone you plan to buy for, and allocate a specific amount of money for each person. Consider giving thoughtful, homemade gifts or focusing on experiences rather than expensive material items. If you're shopping for a large group, set a limit on the amount you'll spend per person, or try a "Secret Santa" gift exchange to keep costs down.

2. Save on Holiday Décor

Decorating your home for Christmas can be a fun and festive way to celebrate, but the costs of ornaments, lights, and other decorations can quickly add up. To stick to your budget, consider reusing decorations from previous years or making your own. For example, you can create handmade garlands, ornaments, and wreaths using materials like pinecones, ribbons, or dried fruits. You can also shop at discount stores, thrift shops, or online marketplaces for budget-friendly decorations. Another way to save money is to purchase items after the holiday season, when stores often offer deep discounts on décor for the following year.

3. Plan for Holiday Meals and Events

Holiday meals and gatherings are often the centerpiece of Christmas celebrations, but hosting can get expensive. Start by planning your menu ahead of time and creating a shopping list to avoid impulse purchases. If you're hosting a big family dinner, consider asking guests to bring a dish to share, or plan a potluck-style gathering to save on the overall cost. If you're attending holiday events like office parties or family gatherings, set a limit on how much you'll spend on food, drink, and gifts. For events such as dinners at home or a New Year's Eve celebration, make sure to plan out your costs for catering, venue rentals, and any entertainment you may want to include.

4. Keep Track of Expenses

Once you have a budget set, it's crucial to keep track of your expenses to avoid overspending. Use a budgeting app or a simple spreadsheet to record every purchase and make sure you stay within your budget. If you're purchasing gifts or decorations in-store, keep receipts, and monitor your bank statements to ensure that you're sticking to the plan. Regularly checking your spending will help you make adjustments throughout the month, preventing any surprises as you get closer to Christmas.

Creating a Personalized Christmas Checklist

A personalized checklist is one of the most effective tools for staying organized and ensuring that you don't miss any important holiday tasks. Whether you prefer pen and paper or a digital planner, creating a comprehensive checklist will help you stay on track and reduce the stress of juggling multiple responsibilities.

1. Gift Shopping Checklist

    Create a list for each person you need to buy gifts for, including specific ideas, prices, and whether you've already purchased the item. This will help you keep track of your spending and prevent you from doubling up on gifts or forgetting someone entirely. As you buy gifts, check off each name, and make sure you've included all details (such as wrapping or delivery instructions). A gift checklist also helps you stay organized when shopping both in-store and online.

2. Event Planning and Scheduling

Make a checklist for all of the events and gatherings you'll be hosting or attending during the holiday season. This includes family dinners, office parties, church services, and community events. For each event, list the necessary items—such as invitations, food preparation, decorations, and entertainment—and assign deadlines to each task. If you're hosting, make a guest list, check the RSVPs, and plan out logistics for seating, meals, and any gifts or party favors you want to distribute. Having a clear schedule will ensure that you don't overcommit or forget any important details.

3. Home Décor and Setup

   When decorating your home, create a checklist of all the areas you want to decorate, such as the tree, the mantelpiece, dining areas, and outdoor spaces. Include any new items you want to purchase or ideas you want to try this year. By breaking down the décor process into manageable steps, you'll be able to enjoy the experience without rushing or feeling overwhelmed. If you have young children, consider giving them age-appropriate tasks, such as helping to decorate the tree or putting up stockings. Make sure to allow time to clean the house and prepare it for guests, as a tidy home will set the right festive mood.

4. Holiday Meals and Treats

If you're planning to cook or bake, create a detailed list of the recipes you'll need to prepare and the ingredients required. Include any special holiday meals you want to serve, from appetizers to main courses and desserts. If you're not preparing the meals yourself, create a checklist of what you need to buy or pick up. Be sure to include any dietary preferences or restrictions to accommodate all your guests.

Overall, planning the perfect Christmas requires organization, time management, and budgeting. By starting early, setting realistic expectations, and using checklists, you can reduce the stress that often accompanies the holiday season.

With a clear plan in place, you'll have more time to focus on what truly matters—spending quality time with loved ones and creating lasting memories.

CONCLUSION

Reflecting on the Holiday Season

As the holiday season draws to a close, it's important to take a moment to reflect on what makes Christmas so special and how we can carry the spirit of this magical time with us throughout the year. Whether through cherished memories, meaningful traditions, or acts of kindness, Christmas has a profound way of reminding us of the beauty of life's simplest joys and the importance of love, compassion, and togetherness.

In this conclusion, we reflect on the significance of the holiday season, explore how we can maintain the warmth of

Christmas all year long, and offer a final wish for a joyous and magical holiday.

Reflecting on the Holiday Season

Christmas is a time of reflection, a moment when we pause from the hustle and bustle of daily life to reconnect with what truly matters. It's a season that encourages us to focus on the deeper meanings behind the traditions we uphold—whether it's the gift of giving, the joy of family gatherings, or the act of sharing a holiday meal.

As we celebrate with loved ones, we're reminded of the importance of human connection. The magic of Christmas lies in its ability to bring people together, fostering an atmosphere of warmth, love, and generosity.

These are the moments that stay with us long after the tinsel is packed away and the lights are turned off. It's a time to pause and appreciate the people in our lives—whether they are near or far—and to reflect on what we've learned over the past year.

The holiday season also offers a chance for renewal and hope. It allows us to reset and look forward to the future with a renewed sense of purpose and optimism. The spirit of Christmas is not just about what happens on December 25th—it's about embracing the values of kindness, gratitude, and community every day of the year.

At the heart of it all, Christmas is a reminder to take joy in the present moment, to be present with those we love, and to cherish the experiences we share with others. The laughter of children opening gifts, the comforting scent of freshly baked cookies, the glow of a well-decked Christmas tree—these are the fleeting moments that make Christmas unforgettable.

Carrying the Spirit of Christmas Throughout the Year

Though Christmas may be a once-a-year celebration, its spirit can live with us long after the season ends. The lessons and values we embrace during the holidays—love, kindness, generosity, and togetherness—can serve as a guiding light throughout the year, making every season brighter and more meaningful.

The Ultimate Christmas Treasury

1. Acts of Kindness

    One of the most beautiful aspects of Christmas is the tradition of giving—whether it's gifts, time, or acts of service. This generosity doesn't have to be confined to December. Small acts of kindness can be done year-round, from helping a neighbor with groceries to volunteering at a local shelter. Carrying forward this spirit of giving, even in small ways, can have a ripple effect on your community and make the world a better place.

2. Maintaining Family Traditions

    While Christmas traditions are often the most prominent, families can carry these traditions beyond the holiday season. Family dinners, game nights, or outings can become regular occurrences throughout the year, fostering deeper connections and creating cherished memories. Additionally, the values instilled through these traditions—such as gratitude, respect, and support for one another—can strengthen the bonds between family members and ensure the spirit of Christmas is present in everyday life.

3. Gratitude and Mindfulness

Christmas encourages a time of reflection and gratitude for the blessings in our lives. We can carry this sense of gratitude forward by incorporating mindfulness practices into our daily routines. Taking a moment each day to reflect on what we're thankful for, practicing generosity, or simply being present for others can help keep the holiday spirit alive in our hearts year-round.

4. Spreading Joy and Love

The joy we feel during the Christmas season doesn't have to fade after the New Year. Whether through simple gestures like sending a card, reaching out to a friend in need, or sharing a meal, spreading joy can brighten someone's day and remind them that they're loved. Keeping this spirit of joy alive helps foster a world that's connected through empathy, kindness,

The Ultimate Christmas Treasury

and shared human experiences.

A Final Wish for a Joyful and Magical Holiday

As you close this book and prepare for the holidays ahead, I offer this final wish: may your Christmas be filled with joy, warmth, and connection. May you find peace in the moments of quiet reflection and excitement in the celebrations with loved ones. Let your heart be open to the magic of the season and the beauty of the world around you, for Christmas is not just a day, but a state of mind that we can carry forward throughout the year.

May your home be filled with the laughter of family and friends, the aroma of festive meals, and the glow of love that shines brighter than any holiday light. May you find joy in the small things, whether it's the first snowflake of the season, the sound of Christmas carols, or the sparkle in a child's eyes as they unwrap a gift.

Above all, may the true meaning of Christmas resonate with you long after the season has passed: that love is the greatest gift of all. It is through love that we experience the fullness of life, and through our connections with others that we truly find the magic of Christmas.

So, whether you're celebrating with a grand feast or enjoying a quiet moment by the fire, take a deep breath and soak in the beauty of the season. Allow the spirit of Christmas to remind you that joy, love, and kindness are gifts we can give all year long.

Wishing you a Christmas filled with warmth, wonder, and love, and may the memories you create this holiday season last for a lifetime.

By reflecting on the true essence of Christmas, carrying its spirit into the new year, and staying connected with the people and traditions that matter most, we ensure that the magic of the season never fades. Instead, it lives on in our hearts, inspiring us to spread joy, kindness, and love throughout every day of the year.